Different Sizes

Which picture is a **different** size?
Draw a circle around the one that is different.

Same Size

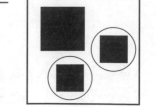

Which two pictures in each box are the **same** size?
Draw circles around the two that are the same size.

Smallest Size

Name _____

12 Answers   Right _____

Which picture in each box is the **smallest**?
Draw a circle around the smallest picture in each box.

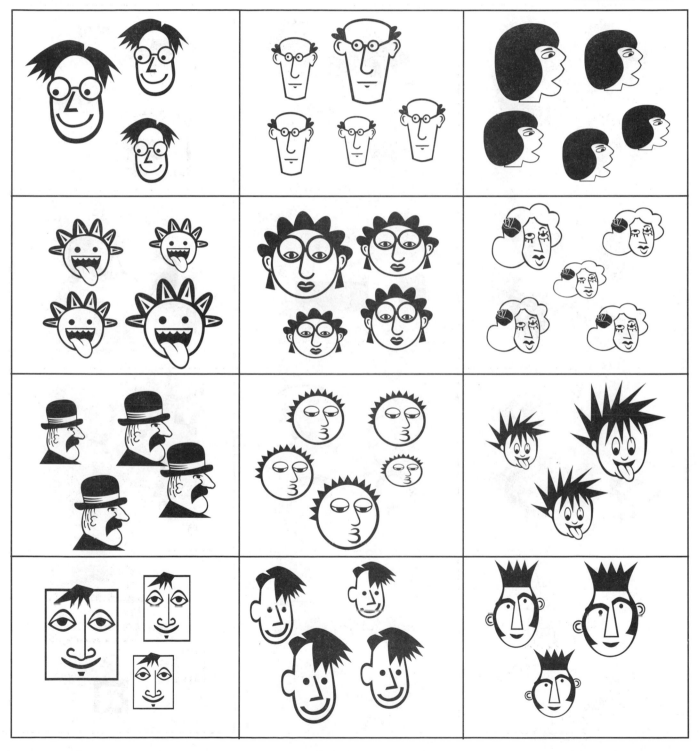

Largest Size

Which picture in each box is the **largest**?
Draw a circle around the largest picture in each box.

4

Circles

Name _____

12 Answers   Right _____

Circle

A circle does not have any corners.
It is round and comes in all sizes.
Draw an **X** on your answer in each box.

Find the circle.		
Which picture has a circle?		
Which circle is different?		
Which two circles are the same?		

Squares

12 Answers   Right _____

Square

A square has four sides and four cornes.
A square is the same on all sides and corners.
Draw an **X** on your answer in each box.

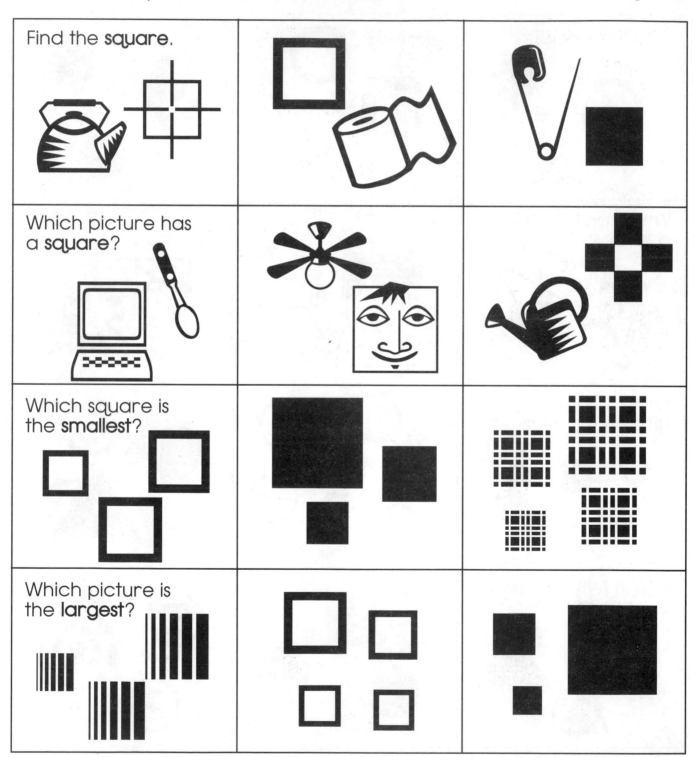

Find the **square**.

Which picture has a **square**?

Which square is the **smallest**?

Which picture is the **largest**?

Triangles

Triangle

A triangle has three sides and three corners.
Triangles come in all sizes.
Draw an **X** on your answer in each box.

Find the **triangle**.		
Which picture has a **triangle**?		
Which triangle is a **different** size?		
Which **two** triangles are the **same** size?		

Rectangles

12 Answers   Right _____

Rectangle

A rectangle has four sides and four corners.
The **opposite** sides on a rectangle are the same length.
Draw an **X** on your answer in each box.

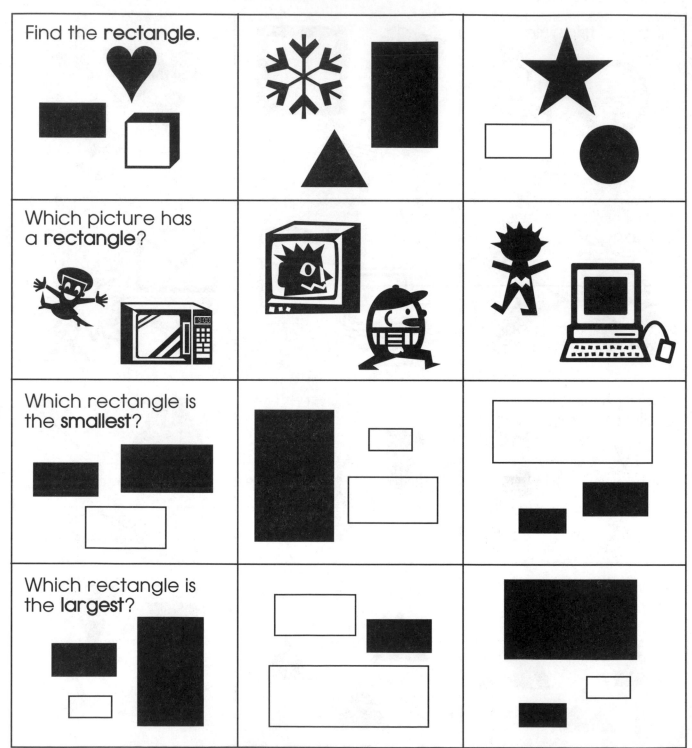

Find the **rectangle**.

Which picture has a **rectangle**?

Which rectangle is the **smallest**?

Which rectangle is the **largest**?

Name _____

Each box has different pictures.
Draw a circle around the picture
that has only **one**.

1 one

Draw a circle around the pictures
that make a set of **two**.

2 two

Trace the numbers.

1 1 1 1 1   2 2 2 2 2

Numbers 3 and 4

Name _____

12 Answers   Right _____

Each box has different pictures.
Draw a circle around the pictures
that make a set of **three**.

3 three

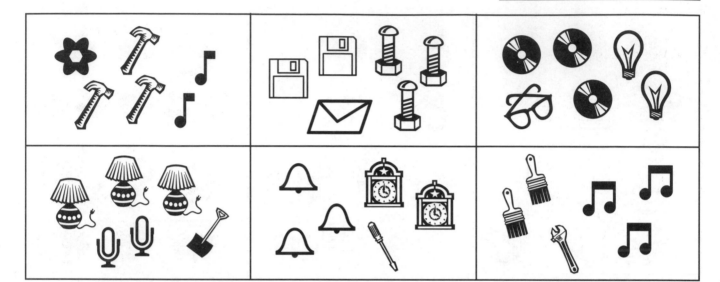

Draw a circle around the pictures
that make a set of **four**.

4 four

Trace the numbers.

3 3 3 3   **4** 4 4 4

_____   _____

10   FS-23231 Skill Drill Math Readiness, Addition, Subtraction

Name _____

12 Answers   Right _____

Each box has different pictures.
Draw a circle around the pictures
that make a set of **five**.

5 five

Draw a circle around the pictures
that make a set of **six**.

6 six

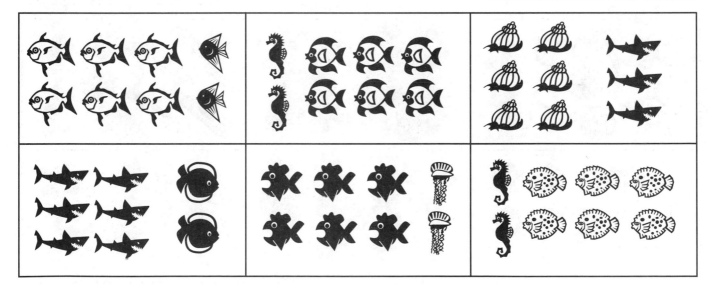

Trace the numbers.

5 5 5 5   **6** 6 6 6

Numbers 7 and 8

Name _____

12 Answers   Right _____

Each box has different pictures. Draw a circle around the pictures that make a set of **seven**.

7 seven

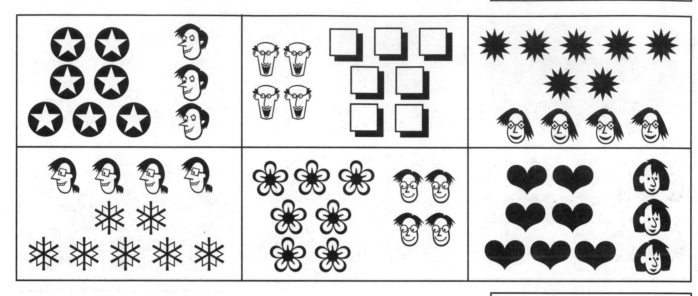

Draw a circle around the pictures that make a set of **eight**.

8 eight

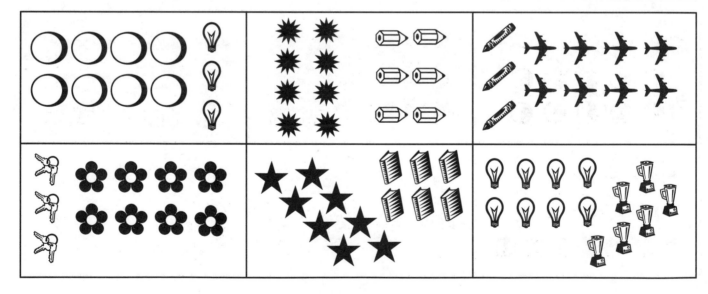

Trace the numbers.

7 7 7 7 7   8 8 8 8

12   FS-23231 Skill Drill Math Readiness, Addition, Subtraction

Numbers 9 and ten

Name _____

12 Answers   Right _____

Each box has different pictures.
Draw a circle around the pictures that
make a set of **nine**.

9 nine

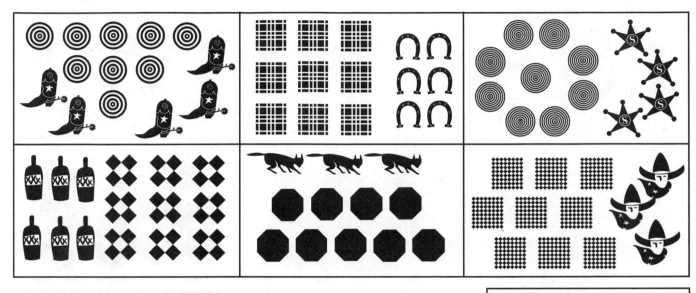

Draw a circle around the pictures that
make a set of **ten**.

10 ten

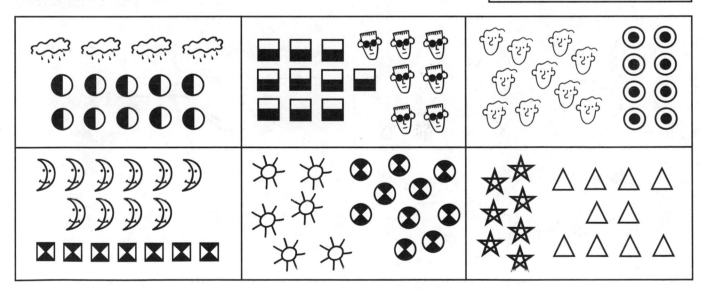

Trace the numbers.

9 9 9 9   10 10 10 10

Number Picture Review

Name _____

Draw a circle around the picture
that matches the number in each box.

▲▲▲ ▲▲▲	**5**	(squirrels)	
(rabbits)	**6**	(snowflakes)	
(swans)	**3**	(stars)	
(squares)	**2**	(elephants)	
(frogs)	**8**	(crosses)	
(mosquitoes)	**10**	(star circles)	
(peace hands)	**4**	(snakes)	
(airplanes & ladybugs)	**9**	(airplanes)	
(butterflies)	**7**	(pencils)	
(dolphin)	**1**	(hearts)	
(flowers)	**8**	(spiders)	
(snails)	**4**	(stars)	
(circles & ladybugs)	**9**	(stars)	
(rabbits)	**5**	(flowers)	

14

Numbers 1 to 5

Practice writing each number.

1   **2**   **3**   **4**   **5**

1   2   3   4   5

1   2   3   4   5

one

This is a swimming fish.
There is **one** fish.

1

two 

These kites are flying.
There are **two** kites.

_____

three 

These flowers are growing in a garden.
There are **three** flowers.

_____

four

These bowls are full of hot soup.
There are **four** bowls.

_____

five

These hearts are in a line.
There are **five** hearts.

_____

Numbers 1 to 5

Practice writing each number.

1   2   3   4   5

1   2   3   4   5

1   2   3   4   5

How many? Circle the number.

one	♥	1 2 3 4 5
four	✳ ✳ ✳ ✳	1 2 3 4 5
two	● ●	1 2 3 4 5
three	■ ■ ■	1 2 3 4 5
two	▲ ▲	1 2 3 4 5
five	✿ ✿ ✿ ✿ ✿	1 2 3 4 5
one	✺	1 2 3 4 5
four	✴ ✴ ✴ ✴	1 2 3 4 5
three	❄ ❄ ❄	1 2 3 4 5

Name _____

38 Answers   Right _____

five _____   ✳ ✳ ✳ ✳ ✳   5
                    ✳ ✳ ✳
_____   ✳ ✳ ✳ ✳   _____
                    ✳
_____   ✳ ✳   _____

_____   _____

_____   ♥ ♥   _____
                    ♥ ♥ ♥ ♥
_____   ♥   _____
                    ♥ ♥ ♥
_____   ♥ ♥ ♥ ♥ ♥   _____

_____   ■   _____
                  ■ ■ ■
_____   ■ ■ ■ ■ ■   _____
                    ■ ■
_____   ■ ■ ■ ■   _____

_____   ✸ ✸ ✸ ✸   _____
                    ✸ ✸
_____   ✸ ✸ ✸ ✸ ✸   _____
                    ✸ ✸ ✸
_____   ✸   _____

Numbers 6 to 10

Name _____

Answers   Right _____

Practice writing each number.

6   **7**   **8**   **9**   **10**

6   7   8   9   10

6   7   8   9   10

How many?

six	○ ○ ○ ○ ○ ○	6	six
seven	○ ○ ○ ○ ○ ○ ○	7	
eight	○ ○ ○ ○ ○ ○ ○ ○	8	
nine	○ ○ ○ ○ ○ ○ ○ ○ ○		
ten	○ ○ ○ ○ ○ ○ ○ ○ ○ ○		

18

Numbers 6 to 10

Name _____

13 Answers   Right _____

Practice writing each number.

6	7	8	9	10
6	7	8	9	10
6	7	8	9	10

How many?

seven	▲ ▲ ▲ ▲ ▲ ▲ ▲	6 7 8 9 10
nine	✿ ✿ ✿ ✿ ✿ ✿ ✿ ✿	6 7 8 9 10
six	❀ ❀ ❀ ❀ ❀ ❀	6 7 8 9 10
eight	○ ○ ○ ○ ○ ○ ○	6 7 8 9 10
ten	☆ ☆ ☆ ☆ ☆ ☆ ☆ ☆ ☆	6 7 8 9 10
six	✿ ✿ ✿ ✿ ✿ ✿	6 7 8 9 10
eight	✸ ✸ ✸ ✸ ✸ ✸ ✸ ✸	6 7 8 9 10
nine	❄ ❄ ❄ ❄ ❄ ❄ ❄ ❄ ❄	6 7 8 9 10

19   FS-23231 Skill Drill Math Readiness, Addition, Subtraction

Number 1 to 10

10 Answers   Right _____

Review how many?

five   🐟 🐟 🐟 🐟 🐟

1	2	3	4	5
6	7	8	9	10

three   🐚 🐚 🐚

1	2	3	4	5
6	7	8	9	10

four   🐟 🐟 🐟 🐟

1	2	3	4	5
6	7	8	9	10

eight   🪼 🪼 🪼 🪼 🪼 🪼 🪼 🪼

1	2	3	4	5
6	7	8	9	10

ten   🐴 🐴 🐴 🐴 🐴 🐴 🐴 🐴 🐴 🐴

1	2	3	4	5
6	7	8	9	10

seven   🐚 🐚 🐚 🐚 🐚 🐚 🐚

1	2	3	4	5
6	7	8	9	10

six   🐬 🐬 🐬 🐬 🐬 🐬

1	2	3	4	5
6	7	8	9	10

nine   🦑 🦑 🦑 🦑 🦑 🦑 🦑 🦑 🦑

1	2	3	4	5
6	7	8	9	10

two   🐡 🐡

1	2	3	4	5
6	7	8	9	10

one   🐡

1	2	3	4	5
6	7	8	9	10

Name _____

12 Answers   Right _____

Trace each number word and numeral.
Then draw enough circles in each box to match the number.

one 1	two 2	three 3
four 4	five 5	six 6
seven 7	eight 8	nine 9
ten 10	eleven 11	twelve 12

21   FS-23231 Skill Drill Math Readiness, Addition, Subtraction

Numbers 1 to 5

Name _____

20 Answers   Right _____

There are   2 little stars
There are   2 big stars

2 and 2 are 4

There are   3 balls with stripes
There are   2 balls with dots

3 and 2 are 5

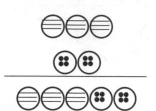

Write the numbers for each story problem.

+  + 1    +    +

Add

	a.	b.	c.	d.	e.	f.
1.	1 + 1 = 2	2 + 1	1 + 2	1 + 3	2 + 2	2 + 3
2.	3 + 1	4 + 1	1 + 4	3 + 2	2 + 3	2 + 1
3.	2 + 2	3 + 2	1 + 4	1 + 1	2 + 1	2 + 3

FS-23231 Skill Drill Math Readiness, Addition, Subtraction

Numbers 1 to 7

Answers   Right _____

Write the numbers in each box.

   and 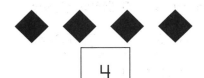 are 4

and

and   are

and   are

	3		3
+ ★★★	+ 3	+ ★★	+ 2
★★★★★★	6	★★★★★	

Addition

Name _____

35 Answers   Right _____

Add:

	a.	b.	c.	d.	e.	f.
1.	4 + 2	6 + 1	2 + 5	3 + 2	1 + 6	1 + 1
2.	2 + 4	5 + 1	5 + 2	2 + 2	2 + 3	1 + 4
3.	1 + 5	1 + 1	5 + 1	1 + 4	1 + 3	4 + 2
4.	2 + 1	6 + 1	4 + 2	1 + 5	1 + 2	5 + 1
5.	1 + 4	4 + 1	2 + 5	3 + 2	1 + 6	6 + 1
6.	2 + 2	3 + 1	2 + 2	5 + 2	3 + 3	4 + 2

24

Numbers 1 to 10

Name _____

Answers   Right _____

Write the numbers in each box.

and ⬜ and ⬜ are ⬜

and ⬜ and ⬜ are ⬜

and ⬜ and ⬜ are ⬜

and ⬜ and ⬜ are ⬜

and ⬜ and ⬜ are ⬜

and ⬜ and ⬜ are ⬜

and ⬜ and ⬜ are ⬜

and ⬜ and ⬜ are ⬜

There are 4 balls here.

○ ○ ○ ●

⬜ ball is black

⬜ are white

⬜ and ⬜ are ⬜

There are 9 hearts here.

♥ ♥ ♥ ♥ ♥ ♡ ♡ ♡ ♡

⬜ hearts are black

⬜ hearts are white

⬜ and ⬜ are ⬜

Addition
Sums to 10

Name _____

36 Answers   Right _____

Add:

	a.	b.	c.	d.	e.	f.
1.	4 + 2	8 + 1	3 + 2	2 + 2	1 + 7	5 + 1
2.	2 + 4	2 + 5	1 + 8	3 + 1	1 + 9	2 + 3
3.	6 + 2	1 + 6	9 + 1	2 + 6	5 + 2	4 + 1
4.	7 + 3	4 + 6	5 + 5	5 + 3	7 + 2	1 + 2
5.	2 + 7	4 + 3	3 + 4	6 + 3	4 + 4	1 + 8
6.	2 + 8	3 + 3	3 + 6	4 + 5	5 + 4	6 + 3

26

Story Problems

Numbers 1 to 10

Fill in the blanks and add.

There are 4 black triangles.
There are 5 white triangles.

▲ ▲ ▲ ▲   △ △ △ △ △

There are _____ black triangles.

There are _____ white triangles.

There are _____ triangles.

Donald has 2 blocks.
Mary has 6 blocks.

Donald and Mary have

_____ blocks together.
$$\begin{array}{r} 2 \\ +\ 6 \\ \hline \end{array}$$

There are 3 big stars.
There are 5 little stars.

★ ★ ★   ✦ ✦ ✦ ✦ ✦

There are _____ big stars.

There are _____ little stars.

There are _____ stars.

Sue has 4 cups.
Jenny has 3 cups.

Sue and Jenny have

_____ cups together.
$$\begin{array}{r} 4 \\ +\ 3 \\ \hline \end{array}$$

There are 6 hearts.
There are 3 flowers

♥ ♥ ♥ ♥ ♥ ♥   ✿ ✿ ✿

There are _____ hearts.

There are _____ flowers.

There are _____ hearts and flowers.

Mike has 9 cats.
John has 1 cat.

Mike and John have

_____ cats together.
$$\begin{array}{r} 9 \\ +\ 1 \\ \hline \end{array}$$

Addition
Sums to 10

36 Answers   Right _____

Add:

	a.	b.	c.	d.	e.	f.
1.	2 + 8	8 + 2	2 + 7	5 + 1	1 + 9	2 + 1
2.	2 + 5	1 + 4	4 + 1	1 + 8	7 + 2	1 + 7
3.	4 + 3	4 + 4	4 + 6	1 + 1	3 + 6	1 + 6
4.	4 + 5	2 + 2	3 + 2	6 + 1	9 + 1	1 + 8
5.	2 + 4	2 + 6	7 + 1	1 + 3	7 + 3	1 + 5
6.	1 + 1	1 + 2	2 + 3	3 + 1	3 + 3	3 + 4

28

Subtraction Story Problems

Remainders 1 to 4

Write the numbers in the blanks.

■■■■ − ■■■ = ■ $\begin{array}{r} 4 \\ -\ 3 \\ \hline 1 \end{array}$ 4 − 3 = 1	●●● −●● = ● ●●● −●● = ● $\begin{array}{r} 6 \\ -\ 4 \\ \hline 2 \end{array}$ 6 − 4 = 2
♥♥ −♥ = ♥ ♥♥ −♥ = ♥ $\begin{array}{r} 4 \\ -\ 2 \\ \hline \end{array}$ ____ − ____ = 2	****− ** =** *** − ** = * $\begin{array}{r} \\ -\ \\ \hline \end{array}$ ____ − ____ = ____
☆☆☆−☆ =☆☆ ☆☆ − ☆ = ☆ $\begin{array}{r} \\ -\ \\ \hline \end{array}$ ____ − ____ = ____	○○○ − ○○○ = ○ ○○○○ −○○○ = $\begin{array}{r} \\ -\ \\ \hline \end{array}$ ____ − ____ = ____
■ ■ − ■ = ■ ■ $\begin{array}{r} \\ -\ \\ \hline \end{array}$ ____ − ____ = ____	♥♥♥ ♥♥ ♥ ♥♥♥ − ♥♥ = ♥ ♥♥♥ ♥ ♥ $\begin{array}{r} \\ -\ \\ \hline \end{array}$ ____ − ____ = ____

FS-23231 Skill Drill Math Readiness, Addition, Subtraction

Subtraction
Remainders 1 t0 8

Name _____

35 Answers   Right _____

Subtract:

	a.	b.	c.	d.	e.	f.
1.	5 − 4	4 − 3	3 − 1	5 − 1	8 − 7	9 − 4
2.	9 − 5	7 − 4	6 − 4	7 − 1	9 − 8	9 − 3
3.	5 − 2	4 − 1	8 − 3	3 − 2	6 − 1	6 − 3
4.	7 − 6	2 − 1	9 − 1	9 − 7	4 − 3	6 − 2
5.	6 − 5	8 − 1	5 − 1	8 − 4	7 − 2	4 − 2
6.	8 − 2	9 − 2	5 − 3	7 − 3	7 − 4	8 − 5

FS-23231 Skill Drill Math Readiness, Addition, Subtraction

Subtraction

Name _____

9 Answers   Right _____

Write the answers in the blanks. Show your work.

1. There are 5 white triangles and 4 dark triangles.

   There are  white triangles.

   There are  dark triangles.

   There is triangle left.

$$\begin{array}{r} 5 \\ -\ 4 \\ \hline 1 \end{array}$$

2. There are 4 cups

   2 cups broke.

   There are _____ cups left.

   _____

3. Mary wants to read 9 pages in her book.

   Mary has read only 4 pages

   Mary needs to read _____ more pages.

   _____

4. John had 7 toy cars.

   He gave 2 of them to Mike.

   John had _____ toy cars left.

   _____

5. Janet had 4 dolls.

   Karen had 3 dolls.

   Janet had _____ more doll than Karen.

   _____

6. Billy ate 8 jellybeans.

   Bob ate 2 jellybeans.

   Billy ate _____ more jellybeans.

   _____

Addition Review
Sums to 10

Name _____

49 Answers   Right _____

Add:

	a.	b.	c.	d.	e.	f.	g.
1.	1 + 1	1 + 3	2 + 2	3 + 4	3 + 1	1 + 4	1 + 2
2.	1 + 2	1 + 5	2 + 4	3 + 3	2 + 8	2 + 3	3 + 5
3.	1 + 6	2 + 5	3 + 6	1 + 8	2 + 7	1 + 9	2 + 6
4.	3 + 7	2 + 8	3 + 2	6 + 1	4 + 2	5 + 3	7 + 2
5.	1 + 7	3 + 1	1 + 6	2 + 8	2 + 2	1 + 3	1 + 1
6.	2 + 5	3 + 3	3 + 5	2 + 7	1 + 4	2 + 4	1 + 8
7.	1 + 5	1 + 9	2 + 3	1 + 2	9 + 1	2 + 6	2 + 1

FS-23231 Skill Drill Math Readiness, Addition, Subtraction

Subtraction Review

Name _____

49 Answers   Right _____

Subtract:

	a.	b.	c.	d.	e.	f.	g.
1.	2 − 1	7 − 2	5 − 1	3 − 2	9 − 4	6 − 3	8 − 2
2.	3 − 1	10 − 2	9 − 3	6 − 5	9 − 8	4 − 2	8 − 7
3.	5 − 3	10 − 4	7 − 1	4 − 1	10 − 8	9 − 6	6 − 1
4.	10 − 1	10 − 7	4 − 3	9 − 7	6 − 2	8 − 1	10 − 3
5.	7 − 6	9 − 1	8 − 3	7 − 5	5 − 4	9 − 2	6 − 4
6.	9 − 5	5 − 2	7 − 3	10 − 9	8 − 5	7 − 4	10 − 5
7.	8 − 4	10 − 6	8 − 6	3 − 1	6 − 2	2 − 1	4 − 3

33   FS-23231 Skill Drill Math Readiness, Addition, Subtraction

Addition/Subtraction
Review

Add:

a.

b.

c.

```
        3           4           7
1.    + 3         + 1         + 2
    _____    _____    _____
```
d. $2 + 3 =$ ___5___
e. $7 + 1 =$ _____

```
        4           4           5
2.    + 4         + 3         + 4
    _____    _____    _____
```
d. $5 + 3 =$ _____
e. $6 + 2 =$ _____

```
        3           1           8
3.    + 1         + 2         + 1
    _____    _____    _____
```
d. $1 + 1 =$ _____
e. $3 + 4 =$ _____

```
        6           5           7
4.    + 2         + 3         + 1
    _____    _____    _____
```
d. $4 + 4 =$ _____
e. $3 + 3 =$ _____

Subtract:

```
        4           7           3
5.    - 1         - 2         - 3
    _____    _____    _____
```
d. $3 - 1 =$ ___2___
e. $7 - 1 =$ _____

```
        4           4           5
6.    - 4         - 3         - 4
    _____    _____    _____
```
d. $5 - 3 =$ _____
e. $6 - 2 =$ _____

```
        3           2           8
7.    - 1         - 1         - 1
    _____    _____    _____
```
d. $1 - 1 =$ _____
e. $4 - 3 =$ _____

Addition/Subtraction

Story Problems

12 Answers   Right _____

Fill in the blanks. Add or subtract. Show your work.

1. Jerry had 6 cookies in his lunch box.

   Jerry ate 3 of the cookies.

   _____ cookies were left in the lunch box.

$$\begin{array}{r} 6 \\ -\ 3 \\ \hline \end{array}$$

2. Pete has 4 marbles.

   Jason has 5 marbles.

   Pete and Jason have _____ marbles.

$$\begin{array}{r} 4 \\ +\ 5 \\ \hline \end{array}$$

3. Jenny jumped rope 7 times.

   Mary jumped rope 3 times.

   Jenny jumped rope _____ more times than Mary.   _____

4. Bobby has 4 blue books.

   He has 2 red books

   Bobby has _____ books.   _____

5. Mark read 2 pages in his story book on Monday.

   He read 5 more pages on Tuesday.

   Mark read _____ pages.   _____

6. Paul has 9 cents.

   Jim has 2 cents.

   Paul has _____ more cents than Jim.   _____

Subtraction/ Proving Your Answer

Name _____

33 Answers   Right _____

Subtract and prove:

	a.	b.	c.	d.	e.	f.

1.
a. $6 - 3 = 3$
b. Proof $3 + 3 = 6$
c. $5 - 2 = 3$
d. Proof $2 + 3$
e. $9 - 8$
f. Proof $+ 1 = 9$

2.
a. $8 - 6$
b. $6 + = 8$
c. $8 - 5$
d. $5 + = 8$
e. $10 - 7$
f. $+$

3.
a. $7 - 4$
b. $+$
c. $9 - 1$
d. $+$
e. $6 - 5$
f. $+$

4.
a. $9 - 3$
b. $+$
c. $10 - 9$
d. $+$
e. $5 - 3$
f. $+$

5.
a. $9 - 6$
b. $+$
c. $8 - 3$
d. $+$
e. $6 - 2$
f. $+$

6.
a. $8 - 2$
b. $+$
c. $9 - 5$
d. $+$
e. $5 - 4$
f. $+$

7.
a. $6 - 4$
b. $+$
c. $4 - 1$
d. $+$
e. $7 - 3$
f. $+$

Addition
Sums 6 to 13

Name _____

36 Answers   Right _____

Add:

	a.	b.	c.	d.	e.	f.
1.	9 + 1	5 + 2	5 + 5	2 + 7	8 + 3	6 + 4
2.	7 + 6	4 + 9	7 + 5	3 + 7	1 + 8	8 + 5
3.	5 + 1	6 + 3	4 + 8	3 + 9	5 + 7	7 + 1
4.	6 + 5	6 + 6	2 + 8	3 + 5	9 + 2	5 + 6
5.	6 + 7	2 + 6	6 + 1	5 + 8	7 + 4	4 + 5
6.	1 + 5	6 + 2	2 + 9	9 + 3	8 + 2	1 + 6

FS-23231 Skill Drill Math Readiness, Addition, Subtraction

Addition

Story Problems

Name _____

12 Answers   Right _____

Write the answer in the blanks. Show your work.

1. Jim and Ed counted the cars going down the street.
    Ed saw 6 blue cars and Jim saw 5 green cars.
    They saw _____ cars.   _____

2. Jean read for 5 minutes in the morning.
    She read for 7 minutes in the afternoon.
    Jean read for _____ minutes.   _____

3. Nancy and Linda took turns batting the ball.
    Nancy hit the ball 8 times.
    Linda hit it 4 times.
    They hit the ball _____ times.   _____

4. Mike has 3 yellow cars
    and 9 blue cars.
    Mike has _____ cars.   _____

5. Lisa counted the fruit in the bowl.
    She counted 4 apples and 5 bananas.
    Lisa counted _____ pieces of fruit.   _____

6. Joe has 4 pairs of blue socks and
    3 pairs of brown socks.
    Joe has _____ pairs of sox.   _____

Subtraction Review
Minuend 6 to 10

Name _____

35 Answers   Right _____

Subtract:

	a.	b.	c.	d.	e.	f.	g.
1.	6 − 5	8 − 2	9 − 3	7 − 4	10 − 7	8 − 4	7 − 3
2.	9 − 8	10 − 2	6 − 1	8 − 6	6 − 3	7 − 5	9 − 6
3.	10 − 9	8 − 1	9 − 4	6 − 2	7 − 1	10 − 5	9 − 2
4.	7 − 2	10 − 6	8 − 7	9 − 7	7 − 6	9 − 5	8 − 1
5.	10 − 1	8 − 5	10 − 4	7 − 5	10 − 3	9 − 6	7 − 2

Numerals and Number Words 1 to 20

Name _____

Write the **numeral** for each number word.

one	_____	eleven	_____
two	_____	twelve	_____
three	_____	thirteen	_____
four	_____	fourteen	_____
five	_____	fifteen	_____
six	_____	sixteen	_____
seven	_____	seventeen	_____
eight	_____	eighteen	_____
nine	_____	nineteen	_____
ten	_____	twenty	_____

Write the **number word** for each numeral.

4	four	20	_____
6	_____	15	_____
5	_____	9	_____
11	_____	13	_____
8	_____	2	_____
1	_____	14	_____
7	_____	3	_____
10	_____	12	_____
16	_____	19	_____
17	_____	18	_____

Numerals and Number Words

Write the **numeral** for each number word.

twenty	_____	nine	_____	seventeen	_____
nineteen	_____	ten	_____	sixteen	_____
eighteen	_____	eleven	_____	fifteen	_____
thirteen	_____	twelve	_____	fourteen	_____
eight	_____	six	_____	seven	_____
three	_____	five	_____	four	_____
two	_____	one	_____	zero	_____

Write the missing **numbers** by adding across.

	a.	b.	c.
1. $6 + 2 =$ _____	$3 + 4 =$ _____	$5 + 3 =$ _____
2. $16 + 2 =$ _____	$13 + 4 =$ _____	$15 + 3 =$ _____
3. $7 + 1 =$ _____	$2 + 1 =$ _____	$4 + 5 =$ _____
4. $17 + 1 =$ _____	$12 + 1 =$ _____	$14 + 5 =$ _____
5. $1 + 8 =$ _____	$3 + 3 =$ _____	$9 + 1 =$ _____
6. $11 + 8 =$ _____	$13 + 3 =$ _____	$19 + 1 =$ _____

Addition by Pairs
Sums through 20

Name _____

36 Answers   Right _____

Add:

	a.	b.	c.	d.	e.	f.
1.	3 + 4	13 + 4	5 + 1	15 + 1	7 + 2	17 + 2
2.	2 + 1	12 + 1	6 + 3	16 + 3	8 + 2	18 + 2
3.	9 + 1	19 + 1	1 + 4	11 + 4	4 + 5	14 + 5
4.	2 + 6	12 + 6	3 + 3	13 + 3	4 + 3	14 + 3
5.	5 + 2	15 + 2	6 + 2	16 + 2	7 + 1	17 + 1
6.	8 + 1	18 + 1	9 + 1	19 + 1	1 + 8	11 + 8

Addition

- 1 digit and 2 digits
- Sums to 19

Name _____

35 Answers   Right _____

> Remember: 0 means none or nothing
> When we add 0 to a number,
> that number does not change.
>
> $19 + 0 = 19$ $\begin{matrix}19\\ +0\\ \hline 19\end{matrix}$ $\begin{matrix}0\\ +19\\ \hline 19\end{matrix}$ $17 + 0 = 17$ $\begin{matrix}17\\ +0\\ \hline 17\end{matrix}$ $\begin{matrix}0\\ +17\\ \hline 17\end{matrix}$
> $0 + 19 = 19$ $0 + 17 = 17$

Add:

	a.	b.	c.	d.	e.	f.	g.
1.	11 + 2	14 + 1	17 + 2	10 + 3	15 + 4	11 + 3	18 + 0
2.	12 + 4	12 + 3	15 + 1	16 + 1	11 + 4	14 + 4	16 + 2
3.	17 + 1	13 + 4	14 + 5	13 + 3	17 + 0	11 + 7	16 + 3
4.	10 + 2	12 + 5	16 + 0	19 + 0	12 + 2	11 + 1	10 + 1
5.	12 + 6	19 + 0	14 + 3	17 + 1	13 + 5	18 + 1	13 + 6

FS-23231 Skill Drill Math Readiness, Addition, Subtraction

Addition
Story Problems

Read each problem. Fill in the blanks. Show your work.

1. Ellen went to the store.
   She spent 10 cents on chewing gum
   and 5 cents on a cookie.

   How much did she spend all together?

   $$\begin{array}{r} 10 \text{ cents} \\ +5 \text{ cents} \\ \hline \text{cents} \end{array}$$

2. Mary has 6 pink flowers and
   5 red flowers in her garden.

   How many flowers are in the garden?

   $$\begin{array}{r} \text{flowers} \\ +\ \ \text{flowers} \\ \hline \text{flowers} \end{array}$$

3. When Jimmy helped his mother on Monday,
   she gave him 8 cents.
   When he helped on Tuesday, she
   gave him 8 cents more.

   How much money does Jimmy have now?   _____

4. Jenny and Mike counted all toys.
   Jenny counted 7 toys and Mike counted 8 toys.

   How many toys did they count together?   _____

5. Six boys are playing ball.
   Eight girls are jumping rope.

   How many children are playing?   _____

6. At Linda's birthday party
   there were 9 girls and 9 boys.

   How many children came to the party?   _____

7. Four girls and nine boys
   walked to school together.

   How many children walked together?   _____

Subtraction by Pairs

Subtract:

	a.	b.	c.	d.	e.	f.
1.	5 − 2	15 − 2	6 − 1	16 − 1	7 − 3	17 − 3
2.	8 − 5	18 − 5	9 − 4	19 − 4	4 − 3	14 − 3
3.	9 − 9	19 − 9	7 − 6	17 − 6	5 − 3	15 − 3
4.	8 − 8	18 − 8	6 − 5	16 − 5	4 − 2	14 − 2

Review – Subtraction

5.	15 − 12	18 − 12	17 − 13	19 − 16	12 − 11	11 − 10
6.	16 − 14	17 − 16	18 − 15	14 − 12	13 − 11	10 − 10
7.	15 − 13	19 − 12	18 − 13	14 − 11	17 − 15	16 − 11

Addition and Subtraction

Read each problem and write the answer. Show your work.

1. There are 19 girls in Jim's class.
   There are 17 boys.

   How many more girls than boys are in Jim's class?   _____

2. Joe spent 12 cents at one store.
   He spent 7 cents at another store.

   How much did he spend at the two stores?   _____

3. Bertha has 13 cents.
   Lynn has 11 cents

   How much more does Bertha have?   _____

4. Raymond and his father drove 8 miles to the store.
   They drove 11 miles to a friend's house.

   How many miles did they drive all together?   _____

5. Carl is 19 years old.
   His brother Gary is 15 years old.

   How many years older is Carl?   _____

6. Johnny ran 16 laps this morning.
   He ran 11 laps this afternoon.

   Did he run more laps in the morning or afternoon?   _____

   How many more laps did he run in the morning?   _____

7. Eleven boys and seven girls played tag.

   How many children played together?   _____

46   FS-23231 Skill Drill Math Readiness, Addition, Subtraction

Numbers and Numerals
21 to 30

Name _____

38 Answers   Right _____

Write the number word by each numeral.

21 _____twenty-one_____   26 _____

22 _____   27 _____

23 _____   28 _____

24 _____   29 _____

25 _____   30 _____thirty_____

Add:

	a.	b.	c.	d.	e.
1.	24 + 2	28 + 1	22 + 5	27 + 2	25 + 4
2.	23 + 5	21 + 7	26 + 2	22 + 3	21 + 8

Subtract:

	a.	b.	c.	d.	e.
3.	21 − 1	28 − 6	29 − 8	25 − 4	22 − 2
4.	23 − 2	26 − 3	25 − 1	24 − 2	27 − 5
5.	27 − 24	26 − 25	29 − 28	21 − 20	24 − 22
6.	22 − 21	23 − 22	25 − 23	28 − 27	29 − 26

Addition
Review

Name _____

36 Answers   Right _____

Add:

	a.	b.	c.	d.	e.	f.
1.	11 + 6	12 + 5	16 + 3	14 + 4	10 + 4	13 + 6
2.	15 + 3	17 + 2	18 + 1	12 + 7	13 + 5	11 + 4
3.	25 + 44	27 + 22	20 + 27	22 + 35	23 + 46	46 + 40
4.	24 + 32	26 + 21	21 + 25	28 + 21	30 + 42	66 + 13
5.	24 + 24	26 + 23	22 + 22	21 + 14	26 + 53	74 + 20
6.	23 + 65	42 + 23	34 + 32	20 + 23	28 + 11	35 + 50

FS-23231 Skill Drill Math Readiness, Addition, Subtraction

Subtraction
Mixed Review

36 Answers   Right _____

Subtract:

	a.	b.	c.	d.	e.	f.
1.	9 − 5	6 − 4	7 − 1	8 − 2	5 − 3	4 − 1
2.	15 − 2	17 − 6	18 − 5	19 − 4	14 − 2	16 − 5
3.	17 − 13	14 − 11	15 − 13	14 − 12	19 − 17	18 − 13
4.	28 − 6	25 − 4	27 − 5	21 − 1	23 − 2	26 − 2
5.	27 − 24	23 − 22	29 − 26	24 − 21	28 − 27	25 − 24
6.	46 − 22	68 − 25	79 − 28	34 − 23	57 − 22	85 − 21

Addition and Subtraction

Read each problem and write the answer. Show your work.

1. In Mark's class there are 23 boys.
   There are 22 girls.

   How many children are there in Mark's class?   _____

2. In Jim's class there are 25 boys.
   There are 21 girls.

   How many more boys than girls are there in Jim's class?   _____

3. In Janet's class, 18 children like to play
   kickball and 7 children like to play dodgeball.

   How many more children like to play kickball?   _____

4. There were 26 birds on the roof.
   Four birds flew away.

   How many birds were left on the roof?   _____

5. Marsha has 15 goldfish and 4 angelfish.

   How many fish does Marsha have all together?   _____

6. Gary counted 28 blue blocks.
   He counted 25 red blocks.

   How many more blue blocks did Gary count?   _____

7. Sam's ball team had 9 points.
   Adam's team had 7 points.

   How many more points did Sam's team have?   _____

8. The children counted 23 big toys and 24 little toys.

   How many toys did they count all together?   _____

Counting Page

30 Answers   Right _____

Here are the numbers from 1 to 100.

Write the missing numbers in the blanks.

1	2	3	___	5	6	7	8	9	10
___	12	13	14	15	16	17	18	___	20
21	22	23	24	25	26	___	28	29	30
31	___	33	34	35	___	37	38	39	40
41	42	43	44	___	46	47	48	___	50
___	52	53	___	55	56	57	58	59	60
61	62	___	64	65	66	___	68	___	70
71	___	73	74	___	76	77	___	79	80
81	82	83	84	85	___	87	88	89	90
91	92	___	94	95	96	___	98	99	100

Write the numeral for each number word below.

two _____   fifteen _____   thirty _____

twenty-one _____   four _____   eight _____

seven _____   ten _____   eleven _____

Counting by 2's 5's 10's

Name _____

24 Answers   Right _____

Write in the missing numbers.

2's	5's	10's
2	5	10
4	10	20
6	___	___
___	20	40
10	25	50
12	___	___
___	35	___
16	___	80
___	45	90
20	50	___
22	55	110
24	___	120
___	65	___
28	___	___
30	75	150
___	80	___
34	___	170
___	___	___
___	95	190
40	___	___

FS-23231 Skill Drill Math Readiness, Addition, Subtraction

Column Addition
Sums to 12

Name _____

35 Answers   Right _____

Add:

	a.	b.	c.	d.	e.	f.	g.
1.	6 1 + 2	2 7 + 2	1 5 + 2	1 3 + 1	2 4 + 2	4 1 + 2	5 2 + 5
2.	3 2 + 1	3 1 + 3	1 7 + 1	5 1 + 2	2 1 + 5	2 3 + 3	1 4 + 4
3.	4 1 + 5	2 7 + 1	6 3 + 3	4 4 + 3	2 1 + 4	3 2 + 3	4 3 + 4
4.	3 5 + 2	3 4 + 3	2 6 + 1	7 2 + 2	1 1 + 2	5 1 + 1	2 1 + 6
5.	2 2 + 2	3 4 + 4	6 1 + 1	1 7 + 2	3 6 + 3	5 2 + 2	8 2 + 1

Column Addition

Sums 8 to 12

Name _____

49 Answers   Right _____

Add:

	a.	b.	c.	d.	e.	f.	g.
1.	9 1 + 1	1 3 + 7	8 2 + 1	1 5 + 6	5 3 + 3	1 1 + 9	1 2 + 5
2.	2 1 + 8	5 5 + 2	2 6 + 2	4 3 + 5	1 2 + 8	7 3 + 1	5 2 + 4
3.	6 4 + 2	2 1 + 7	2 5 + 3	1 2 + 9	2 3 + 4	1 4 + 6	3 4 + 3
4.	3 4 + 1	2 6 + 3	3 5 + 4	4 4 + 4	4 5 + 1	3 7 + 2	2 2 + 7
5.	2 6 + 1	2 1 + 9	1 1 + 8	1 4 + 5	2 8 + 2	2 5 + 5	1 3 + 6
6.	4 2 + 6	2 2 + 8	1 7 + 3	1 2 + 9	4 1 + 6	2 3 + 7	1 3 + 8
7.	1 6 + 5	1 1 + 9	2 6 + 4	1 7 + 4	1 8 + 3	1 4 + 7	1 9 + 2

54   FS-23231 Skill Drill Math Readiness, Addition, Subtraction

Addition

- Sums to 12
- Using zero

Add:

> Remember: 0 means none or nothing
>   When we add 0 to a number,
>   that number does not change.
>
> $5 + 3 + 0 = 8$ $5 + 0 + 3 = 8$ $0 + 5 + 3 = 8$
>
> $$\begin{array}{r} 5 \\ 3 \\ +\ 0 \\ \hline 8 \end{array} \qquad \begin{array}{r} 5 \\ 0 \\ +\ 3 \\ \hline 8 \end{array} \qquad \begin{array}{r} 0 \\ 5 \\ +\ 3 \\ \hline 8 \end{array}$$

	a.	b.	c.	d.	e.	f.	g.
1.	$\begin{array}{r}4\\2\\+\ 5\\\hline\end{array}$	$\begin{array}{r}5\\5\\+\ 1\\\hline\end{array}$	$\begin{array}{r}0\\4\\+\ 8\\\hline\end{array}$	$\begin{array}{r}2\\6\\+\ 1\\\hline\end{array}$	$\begin{array}{r}2\\1\\+\ 9\\\hline\end{array}$	$\begin{array}{r}3\\5\\+\ 2\\\hline\end{array}$	$\begin{array}{r}4\\0\\+\ 6\\\hline\end{array}$
2.	$\begin{array}{r}0\\4\\+\ 7\\\hline\end{array}$	$\begin{array}{r}3\\3\\+\ 4\\\hline\end{array}$	$\begin{array}{r}1\\7\\+\ 2\\\hline\end{array}$	$\begin{array}{r}0\\3\\+\ 8\\\hline\end{array}$	$\begin{array}{r}0\\3\\+\ 9\\\hline\end{array}$	$\begin{array}{r}9\\1\\+\ 0\\\hline\end{array}$	$\begin{array}{r}3\\6\\+\ 2\\\hline\end{array}$
3.	$\begin{array}{r}0\\6\\+\ 5\\\hline\end{array}$	$\begin{array}{r}0\\8\\+\ 2\\\hline\end{array}$	$\begin{array}{r}0\\2\\+\ 7\\\hline\end{array}$	$\begin{array}{r}2\\3\\+\ 7\\\hline\end{array}$	$\begin{array}{r}3\\4\\+\ 4\\\hline\end{array}$	$\begin{array}{r}4\\4\\+\ 3\\\hline\end{array}$	$\begin{array}{r}2\\7\\+\ 1\\\hline\end{array}$
4.	$\begin{array}{r}4\\2\\+\ 6\\\hline\end{array}$	$\begin{array}{r}3\\8\\+\ 1\\\hline\end{array}$	$\begin{array}{r}2\\5\\+\ 4\\\hline\end{array}$	$\begin{array}{r}3\\5\\+\ 3\\\hline\end{array}$	$\begin{array}{r}0\\2\\+\ 9\\\hline\end{array}$	$\begin{array}{r}2\\3\\+\ 5\\\hline\end{array}$	$\begin{array}{r}5\\1\\+\ 6\\\hline\end{array}$
5.	$\begin{array}{r}2\\1\\+\ 7\\\hline\end{array}$	$\begin{array}{r}1\\2\\+\ 8\\\hline\end{array}$	$\begin{array}{r}1\\9\\+\ 2\\\hline\end{array}$	$\begin{array}{r}1\\4\\+\ 5\\\hline\end{array}$	$\begin{array}{r}2\\6\\+\ 3\\\hline\end{array}$	$\begin{array}{r}9\\2\\+\ 0\\\hline\end{array}$	$\begin{array}{r}2\\1\\+\ 9\\\hline\end{array}$

Column Addition
Sums to 19

Name _____

49 Answers   Right _____

Add:

	a.	b.	c.	d.	e.	f.	g.
1.	9 1 + 9	2 5 + 7	5 5 + 6	8 9 + 1	4 5 + 8	7 9 + 2	1 8 + 5
2.	2 8 + 2	8 5 + 3	5 5 + 4	4 4 + 3	9 7 + 2	6 2 + 9	4 4 + 4
3.	6 6 + 6	2 4 + 8	3 8 + 1	5 9 + 5	5 3 + 9	6 7 + 5	5 7 + 1
4.	7 6 + 2	8 6 + 5	9 6 + 3	3 3 + 8	4 8 + 6	6 3 + 7	4 7 + 6
5.	5 6 + 4	4 9 + 6	7 7 + 3	8 7 + 4	2 4 + 7	8 2 + 7	5 5 + 5
6.	9 5 + 1	3 5 + 9	2 5 + 2	5 8 + 4	6 8 + 3	3 4 + 9	4 6 + 1
7.	1 9 + 3	8 1 + 7	5 2 + 8	6 4 + 2	2 9 + 4	5 4 + 1	3 1 + 8

FS-23231 Skill Drill Math Readiness, Addition, Subtraction

Column Addition

- Sums to 19
- Using zero

Name _____

49 Answers   Right _____

Add:

	a.	b.	c.	d.	e.	f.	g.
1.	0 5 + 3	3 2 + 8	6 3 + 9	7 7 + 4	0 1 + 9	5 7 + 3	2 7 + 6
2.	0 4 + 2	7 5 + 2	6 4 + 0	2 9 + 5	8 5 + 0	3 5 + 5	1 8 + 8
3.	2 7 + 7	9 4 + 1	8 5 + 1	0 1 + 6	3 8 + 4	2 1 + 8	0 9 + 7
4.	1 8 + 6	8 2 + 1	9 3 + 0	6 4 + 3	5 3 + 1	9 2 + 7	0 6 + 6
5.	3 8 + 5	6 2 + 0	5 3 + 2	8 0 + 9	7 6 + 2	9 0 + 6	1 7 + 5
6.	7 6 + 4	2 1 + 1	4 2 + 2	8 1 + 7	5 3 + 8	5 6 + 5	4 4 + 4
7.	6 1 + 0	6 2 + 9	7 3 + 3	6 0 + 8	5 6 + 3	7 5 + 4	9 0 + 7

Column Addition
Story Problems

1. Ben counted 7 bananas, 2 apples,
   and 2 oranges.

   How many pieces of fruit did he count?   _____

2. Paul's school has 3 kickballs, 3 baseballs,
   and 4 volleyballs.

   How many balls are there at Paul's school?   _____

3. Sally has 5 red jellybeans, 4 yellow jellybeans,
   and 2 orange jellybeans.

   How many jellybeans does Sally have?   _____

4. Linda ate 2 pieces of chicken.
   Jill ate 1 piece of chicken.
   Barbara ate 3 pieces of chicken.

   How many pieces of chicken were eaten?   _____

5. Jack played the piano for 5 minutes.
   He read his book for 5 minutes and
   went out to play for 5 minutes.

   How many minutes is that all together?   _____

6. Matt's cat had 3 white kittens,
   2 black kittens, and 2 striped kittens.

   How many kittens were there?   _____

7. Lisa spent 3 cents on gum, 5 cents on peanuts,
   and 5 cents on an apple.

   How much did Lisa spend?   _____

8. Connie's coat has 2 large buttons,
   6 middle sized buttons, and 2 tiny buttons.

   How many buttons are there on Connie's coat?   _____

Addition Facts – Test
4 Minutes

Name _____

42 Answers   Right _____

Add:

	a.	b.	c.	d.	e.	f.	g.
1.	9 + 2	2 + 3	5 + 4	7 + 2	8 + 1	1 + 2	3 + 3
2.	2 + 4	4 + 3	3 + 7	6 + 4	1 + 6	1 + 8	4 + 4
3.	8 + 2	6 + 3	1 + 1	3 + 6	2 + 2	2 + 7	9 + 1
4.	7 + 1	6 + 2	1 + 3	3 + 5	4 + 5	1 + 5	5 + 3
5.	4 + 1	5 + 5	3 + 4	1 + 7	3 + 2	5 + 2	1 + 4
6.	2 + 1	2 + 5	1 + 6	2 + 6	4 + 1	4 + 2	5 + 4

Subtraction Facts – Test
5 Minutes

Name_____

49 Answers   Right _____

Subtract:

	a.	b.	c.	d.	e.	f.	g.
1.	7 − 5	5 − 2	9 − 6	11 − 8	3 − 1	6 − 5	8 − 3
2.	10 − 4	12 − 3	2 − 1	4 − 2	10 − 7	3 − 2	5 − 1
3.	8 − 7	5 − 3	10 − 9	8 − 4	12 − 9	4 − 3	9 − 4
4.	4 − 1	7 − 6	9 − 2	11 − 6	7 − 4	8 − 2	9 − 7
5.	11 − 3	12 − 2	9 − 1	5 − 4	7 − 2	8 − 6	12 − 4
6.	9 − 5	6 − 2	7 − 1	10 − 1	6 − 4	9 − 3	11 − 2

1. Mary saw 6 bluebirds and 4 sparrows in her yard.
   How many birds did Mary see?   _____

2. Jim has 4 blue trucks, 2 red trucks,
   and 7 yellow trucks.
   How many trucks does Jim have?   _____

3. Holly has 8 roses.
   Cindy has 5 roses.
   Holly has how many more roses?   _____

4. John has 6 turtles.
   He gave 2 of them to Ted.
   How many turtles did John have then?   _____

5. Amy spent 12 cents for carrots and
   16 cents for bananas.
   How much did Amy spend?   _____

6. Maria picked 9 flowers.
   Four of her flowers were pink.
   How many of Maria's flowers were not pink?   _____

7. Danny took 11 minutes to walk to the store.
   He took 13 minutes to walk home.
   How many minutes did Danny's trip take?   _____

8. There are 23 girls and
   21 boys in Henry's class.
   How many more girls than boys are in his class?   _____

Addition Review

Name _____

49 Answers   Right _____

Add:

	a.	b.	c.	d.	e.	f.	g.
1.	1 + 5	7 + 2	3 + 3	10 + 4	12 + 7	6 + 5	14 + 4
2.	13 + 5	2 + 9	8 + 3	9 + 7	4 + 7	11 + 6	5 + 9
3.	15 + 2	20 + 7	18 + 1	16 + 2	23 + 6	21 + 8	17 + 1
4.	7 2 + 2	6 1 + 2	3 4 + 4	2 3 + 3	1 2 + 9	5 2 + 4	4 0 + 6
5.	0 5 + 5	7 4 + 0	4 0 + 8	3 4 + 9	6 8 + 3	9 0 + 6	8 5 + 0
6.	21 + 5	34 + 3	22 + 2	46 + 2	35 + 4	47 + 1	23 + 4
7.	44 + 21	55 + 33	32 + 26	36 + 52	61 + 25	83 + 10	74 + 20

62   FS-23231 Skill Drill Math Readiness, Addition, Subtraction

Subtraction Review

Subtract:

	a.	b.	c.	d.	e.	f.	g.
1.	8 − 4	4 − 1	2 − 2	13 − 1	7 − 3	14 − 2	6 − 5
2.	9 − 7	1 − 1	12 − 2	3 − 1	11 − 1	5 − 4	10 − 5
3.	15 − 3	18 − 6	16 − 5	12 − 1	15 − 2	19 − 5	17 − 2
4.	13 − 12	17 − 15	14 − 10	18 − 13	16 − 11	19 − 16	15 − 14
5.	23 − 1	36 − 3	24 − 2	38 − 4	49 − 5	25 − 2	37 − 6
6.	59 − 15	65 − 23	73 − 21	58 − 45	66 − 34	88 − 35	57 − 42
7.	98 − 30	69 − 50	46 − 26	85 − 45	48 − 42	24 − 22	37 − 37

63   FS-23231 Skill Drill Math Readiness, Addition, Subtraction

Addition/Subtraction
Review Test

Name _____

47 Answers   Right _____

Add:

	a.	b.	c.	d.	e.	f.
1.	4 + 3	6 + 2	11 + 12	16 + 13	11 + 17	15 + 3
2.	21 + 7	26 + 2	25 + 44	22 + 22	20 + 27	26 + 21
3.	43 + 41	28 + 21	30 + 42	5 2 + 3	3 1 + 4	2 3 + 6

(row 3, column f.)
7
1
+ 2

4. 3 + 4 = _____   5 + 2 = _____   2 + 3 + 2 = _____

11 + 7 = _____   2 + 1 + 3 = _____

Subtract:

	a.	b.	c.	d.	e.	f.
5.	5 − 2	15 − 2	7 − 6	17 − 6	9 − 4	19 − 4
6.	7 − 1	14 − 2	15 − 13	19 − 17	28 − 6	28 − 2
7.	28 − 27	24 − 21	29 − 25	23 − 21	27 − 22	25 − 22

8. 3 − 2 = _____   9 − 6 = _____   17 − 4 = _____

16 − 14 = _____   26 − 24 = _____

FS-23231 Skill Drill Math Readiness, Addition, Subtraction